Service! Some People Just Don't Get It!

A Simple and Powerful Plan for Creating "Magnetic" Customer Service!

Trapper Woods and Todd Woods

with affection and appreciation for
Bill Woods
and the legacy he left behind

The Proof is Three Generations Strong

WARNING: This book was not written by a Ph.D. and may contain simple ideas you can apply immediately.

NEW YORK

SERVICE! SOME PEOPLE JUST DON'T GET IT!

ISBN: 1-60037-026-8 (Paperback)

Published by:
MORGAN · JAMES
THE ENTREPRENEURIAL PUBLISHER™

Morgan James Publishing, LLC
1225 Franklin Ave Ste 325
Garden City, NY 11530-1693
Toll Free 800-485-4943
www.MorganJamesPublishing.com

Cover and Interior Design by:
Tony Laidig
www.thecoverexpert.com
tony@thecoverexpert.com

In Memory

BILL WOODS

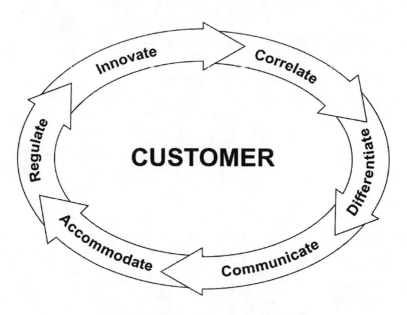

THE CIRCLE OF SERVICE

Foreword

Yesterday I drove up to McDonald's and ordered a coke. The mystery voice at the drive-through said, "I'm sorry, sir, I can't sell you a coke." "Why?" I asked. To which the mystery voice replied, "Our computer is down!" "You mean I can't drive up to the window, hand you $1.69 and you hand me a coke?" "Nope, but if you come inside we can sell you a coke." It was 113 degrees in my hometown of Phoenix that day. I wasn't interested in getting out of the car, so I drove to Taco Bell.

Many people are fed up with the nonsense we often face today when we try to get a little customer service. It doesn't matter whether they are buying low-priced or high-priced services. Many people are often appalled and disappointed at the treatment they receive.

Traditionally there are many establishments in our society that do provide superior service. That's where we go to shop and that's where you go too! These businesses flourish because they apply the principles that are enumerated in this book. If your own business is not flourishing, we encourage you to take a little time to compare your service process with the ideas on the following pages. Then fill in the gaps. We are confident your business can and will flourish too.

Table of Contents

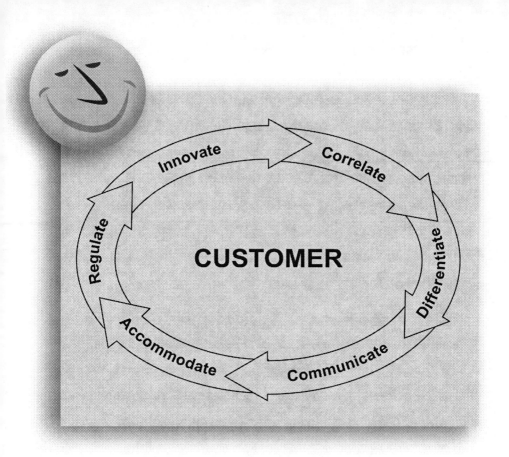

Playing to the Crowd

It was March 12, 1991. I'm reminiscing about that night. We attended a concert by the Phoenix Jazz Band and watched my father, the perfectionist, performing with his sax and clarinet. He was 83.

It was he who tutored me in the art of Magnetic Customer Service and led me into a customer service career of 38 years. This book is about what we learned not to do, what we learned to do, and how we did it. It is, in the expression of a musician, "how to play to the crowd."

I believe whether we become service stars or not depends on these personal or organizational qualities. They are: 1) a fondness for people, 2) a commitment to serve, and 3) relentless tenacity. All the training and good service ideas in the world won't mean much if these qualities are missing. These values were lived by my customer service tutor, by any effective employee who worked for us, and by any effective business agent with whom we competed.

My service schooling started in my youth when my dad and I were heading into Idaho to do some fishing on the North Fork of the Snake River. We stopped for gas at a service station in Pocatello, Idaho. (This was in the era when service stations actually gave service.) The attendant, who was busy pumping gas into another car, looked our way and shouted, "I'll be with you in a minute."

"There! Did you see that?" my dad said enthusiastically. "That's good customer service. Remember, even if you are busy, always acknowledge the new customer's presence promptly!"

From that moment on, my father would seize every teaching opportunity to make a point about customer service. This tutoring started long before I entered the family business and continued throughout our entire career together. If we were in a restaurant, a hotel, or on an airplane, he'd always point out a feature he liked or didn't like about the service we were experiencing.

This book is based on principles learned, taught, and practiced in our business for 38 years. These same principles were successfully applied by my son Todd in his Jamba Juice stores in Phoenix, Arizona, prior to his selling them to become a marketing consultant.

What's Your Favorite Channel?

The setting for an evening of dining was exquisite. Situated high in the Wasatch Mountains of Utah, the air was clear and cool with the gentle, fresh aroma of pine perfume. As we walked toward the lodge, the setting sun was casting long shadows across the rugged slopes. The snow-capped peaks were illuminated with a pastel pink glow. What a perfect evening it was to be dining with our good friends, Stuart and Elaine Cannon. We'd been friends for a long time and loved being in their company.

We settled into the candlelight comfort of the lodge restaurant and engaged in casual conversation. Our plates were not disappointing. The food was well presented. It was hot, tasty, colorful and artistically arranged. We savored it! As we were walking back to our car underneath a sky filled with unusually bright stars, Stuart commented on how great both the food and the service were. I told him I had a different impression. While it is true the food was excellent, I disagreed about the service.

"But why?" asked Stuart. "The food server was very polite and his timing was excellent."

"Everything you say is true," I said. "But what to me is the most important component of customer service was missing."

"What's that?" he said.

"Channel two," I responded.

"Channel two?" he queried.

A channel is a means of communication, and customers evaluate service on two channels: channel one, the *transaction* channel and channel two, the *relationship* channel.

The transaction channel is the service provided. The service provided includes everything from arranging for a business loan, a visit to a doctor's office, or being served an ice cream cone.

The relationship channel is the feelings created. The feelings created can range from frustration and anger to joy and bliss. In a nutshell, the relationship channel is the human connection made with the customer.

To put it another way, customer service is not just going through the motions (the transaction channel). It is also about going through the emotions (the relationship channel). Let me say that again . . .

> Magnetic customer service is not just going through the motions. It is also going through the emotions.
>
>

Unfortunately, as machines are used to handle more of the transaction channel, the relationship channel is being diminished and ignored. More and more customers are upset by it. It reminds me of . . .

My Affair with Henry-the-Computer!

It was the kind of day that everyone hates to fly. It was snowy, icy, dark, cold, and inhospitable. You get the picture. I was trying to fly from Chicago O'Hare to Milwaukee, which should have taken a short amount of time, but it was stretched into hours because we had to wait for personnel to de-ice the plane before we could get clearance. When we got to Milwaukee I was completely exhausted. I stood at a carousel waiting for my bag. A large pit was forming in my stomach and with good reason. The last bag came up and it wasn't mine. My heart sank! This was the last thing I wanted to end my day.

I was exhausted and frustrated. I went to United Airline's baggage claim department where a woman was seated behind a computer. She was so robotical it was hard to tell where the computer ended and she began.

She said, very matter-of-factly, "We'll deliver your bag when we find it," and moved on to the next customer.

"Wait a minute!" I said. "What happens if it's 11 or 12 o'clock at night and I still don't have my bag?"

"Call this number," she said and handed me a piece of paper.

Well, it was very late at night and I had still not received my bag, so I called the number. The voice on the other end of the line said, "Hi, my name is Henry. I'm a computer. Let me see if I can help you find your bag. Now, please say your name slowly and clearly."

I did.

Henry said, "I'm sorry, I don't understand. Please say your name again."

After three tries, Henry-the-Computer finally understood my name. He then asked for more information such as city of origin, flight number, etc. I had to speak slowly to answer every question. In most cases I had to try more than once before the computer understood me.

Henry-the-Computer then said, "Wait just a moment. Let me see if I can locate your bag."

After waiting several minutes Henry said, "I'm sorry, I can't locate your bag. Please call this number."

I called the number and got another computer that said, "All of our agents are busy. Please hold."

By then I was very irritated. And what irritated me most about the whole situation was when the computer told me it was "sorry." What? Computers can't be sorry. They don't have emotions! They can only deliver service on the transaction channel, not the relationship channel. That ended my affair with Henry, and I hope I never speak to him, or shall I say "it," again.

Organizations used to use machines to back up people. Now they use people to back up machines. The more companies do that, the more the relationship channel disappears. The more the relationship channel disappears, the bigger the opportunity for you and your company to fill the void. But to deliver magnetic customer service you must remember that there are . . .

Two Channels for Two Styles

One mistake many companies make in serving customers is delivering on only one of the channels. Good customer service means different things to different people. Let's take, for example, someone who goes into a restaurant. Some are really only concerned about getting good-tasting food, delivered quickly (the transaction).

Others care more about a clean environment. If the place isn't clean, they are not happy (the transaction).

Some people want friendly conversation from the server, and love the server who engages in genuine communication with them (the relationship). Some customers don't want any conversation at all.

These differences are driven by two different customer styles. These styles are monochronic and polychronic. To some extent, people lean toward one of these styles. To the extent they lean toward a certain style, each customer defines and experiences excellent customer service differently.

A monochronic style is one where essentially one event or activity occurs at a time, typically to completion. This style involves a structured, more defined mode of operation. Essentially, this style is task-oriented. Does this sound like you?

Or, perhaps you are more polychronic. A polychronic style is one where several activities occur simultaneously. This style involves an unstructured, flexible mode of operation and is relationship oriented.

The following lists of characteristics will give you an idea of what I mean.

Monochronic Style

Task-oriented

Do activities in a linear manner

Socially reserved

Limited expression of feelings/emotions

Focused on respect, strategy, and systems

Individual-oriented

Formal

Direct

Fixed

Focused on the goal

Customers who tend toward a monochronic style are more concerned with the transaction channel and want—and even expect—the transaction to be executed perfectly.

Polychronic Style

Relationship-oriented

Socially expressive

Open expression of feelings

Focused on trust, sensitivity and communication

People-oriented

Informal

Indirect

Flexible

Multitasking

Focused on the process

Customers who lean more toward a polychronic style see the relationship channel as extremely important. To them, if the relationship channel is missing, it makes no difference how flawlessly the transaction was executed.

Understanding and respecting different styles makes a world of difference not only in delivering magnetic customer service but also in the workplace, which is really just in-house magnetic service. See how critical it can be when . .

She Wasn't Even "Broken"

I worked with a telemarketing company. The manager of the sales team was monochronic. One of his top salespersons was polychronic. She had the gift of reading a customer's style very quickly and adapting accordingly. She was excellent at delivering service in the relationship channel.

The manager decided she needed to be fixed. Never mind the fact that customers loved her. He set her up on a rigid structure requiring her to make more calls in shorter periods of time, keep more detailed records, and file what she felt were complicated reports. In short, he wanted her to be monochronic in style.

What do you think she did? She quit! And the company lost their best salesperson. But that's not all the company lost. They lost someone who really knew how to deliver on the relationship channel. This manager just didn't get it.

Here's an example of how one employee of Day-Timers, Inc. gets it, and it's . . .

Not a Shaggy Dog Story

One day, Day-Timers, Inc. received a binder returned by a really unhappy customer. It seems her dog chewed her luxurious calfskin binder to shreds. It wasn't the company's fault. But what do you think the company did? That's right, they replaced the binder.

⊷ 10 ⊷

> "Consider the benefits of managing the relationship. If your customers don't like you, the odds are 100 to 1 they aren't going to like your service."
>
> *Price Pritchitt*

Now, the best rule when fixing a problem is don't just fix the problem, fix it with a "perk." So not only did the company replace the new binder, they also sent the customer a dog biscuit.

Two weeks later a thank you note appeared. From the dog! All of that information went into the computer. One year later, when it was time to send out the new Day-Timer® calendars, the company sent this customer a second dog biscuit. Sure enough, a thank you note appeared from the dog. This time there was a "p.s." at the bottom of the note. It read, "Got a problem, cat is jealous." So the company sent over a can of cat food.

A third letter appeared, this one written by the owner of the animals thanking Day-Timers for its excellent customer service. However, there was a "p.s." on the bottom of this thank you note that said, "By the way, the dog really didn't write the letters—the cat did."

Do you think this customer will ever buy another brand? Never!!! It's a true story. What a perfect example of a complaint being handled on the relationship channel using a polychronic style. This Day-Timers employee definitely gets it.

How do you know when a customer comes into your store, or begins conducting business with you, which channel is more important to them—the relationship channel or the transaction channel? The answer is—unless they are a repeat customer, you really don't know. So you need to deliver on both channels effectively.

Deliver customer service consistently on both channels and watch your business grow and flourish. That sounds great, but what exactly is customer service?

The True Definition of Customer Service

The common thread that defines companies who "get it" and deliver great customer service, and companies who don't get it and don't deliver, is found in what we believe is the true definition of customer service. Many books teach that customer service is *"meeting or exceeding the customer's expectations."* We disagree. We believe this is only the end result of customer service.

The *"real"* definition of customer service is this: *an internally driven, sincere desire to take care of the customer.* We call this the *"service spirit."*

> The "real" definition of customer service: an internally driven, sincere desire to take care of the customer.

One evening I experienced the service spirit in such a way that I wasn't sure if I was in the . . .

AutoZone or Twilight Zone?

We were having trouble with our newly purchased Hewlett Packard printer from OfficeMax. It was our fault. We had loaded the inkjet cartridges incorrectly. We tried everything to get them back out and nothing worked. We took the printer back to OfficeMax. We were waited on by a nice young man who essentially said, "You've got a problem, and I can't help you." He did make one suggestion though.

"Why not go to AutoZone, pick up a star wrench that will fit this machine, take it apart and fix it yourself?"

We thought we'd give it a try. I'd never shopped at an Auto-Zone before. We pulled up and walked in. I was instantly greeted by a very nice young woman. We told her our problem. She found the wrench we needed.

Just then the store manager came by. He said, "What can I do for you?" She told him what our problem was and he said, "Well, I think I can fix that."

While we watched in amazement, he took the machine apart, put the cartridges in the right place, reassembled the machine, and said, "There's certainly no charge for that."

I said, "Well, I really feel guilty. I need to at least buy something."

He said, "No, no, no, no! That's okay. That's AutoZone service."

However, we did buy something and we will always go back. Isn't it curious that the store where we bought the printer was not the store that helped us? It was fixed by AutoZone. Auto-Zone gets it! So did my dad who always dressed well except when shopping for cars. Then he would go . . .

From Riches to Rags

I mentioned my father in the beginning of this book. He was a detail person when it came to service. One thing he couldn't stand was a service professional who didn't have that inner drive to sincerely please customers. To make sure he never had to deal with such a person, here's how he would shop for a car.

He'd put on the oldest gardening clothes he could find and don his old work boots. He often wouldn't shave either. He intentionally made himself look like he didn't have a dime to his name. Then he would walk into a luxury-car showroom and mosey around looking at the different models. Often, no salesperson would approach him, in which case he would walk out, go down the street, and buy a car from that dealership's competitor. Yes, he really did get it!

He was confident if there was a sincere salesperson on the sales floor, a real service professional, that person would show some interest no matter how he, the customer, looked. As you might guess, dad took pleasure in knowing he could afford any car he wanted. And he wasn't going to allow himself to be served by somebody he would call a hack (an amateur only in it for the commission).

It is easy to spot someone who is only trying to sell you something just for the money. And you don't trust them because you know they don't have your best interest at heart. Yes, we all need to earn a living and we'd like it to be a comfortable living. But customers sense the lack of integrity in the service representative when their primary goal is a paycheck. Perhaps Earl Nightingale put it best when he said . . .

> "Whatever you seek in the form of reward, you must first earn in the service to others."
>
> *Earl Nightingale*

A perfect example of this happened the day I was . . .

Chased by a Flight Attendant

Hiring employees who naturally like to please others, hiring people who have that internally driven desire to promote the well-being of others, is crucial in achieving customer service excellence. It's easy to determine if they've got it or they don't. Just observe them.

For example, I was on a Delta flight between Philadelphia and Chicago. I observed the flight attendants working the cabin. I instantly spotted the one of the three who had the internally driven desire to please and promote the well-being of others. She was engaging the passengers on both the transaction and relationship channels. The other two just seemed to be going through the motions in sort of a ho-hum way.

When I landed in Chicago to make my connection, I took my time meandering to the next gate. To my astonishment, when I got there, the flight attendant who had been on my previous flight, the one I determined as the service pro, was standing by the boarding gate. She had just had me paged and was waiting to hand me my Day-Timer® which I'd left on her flight. With a big smile she handed it to me and said, "Here, Mr. Woods, I think you'll need this."

I was extremely grateful that she took the time to check my itinerary and get my Day-Timer® to me rather than just throw it in the lost and found as the other two flight attendants would have done. *This flight attendant gets it!*

No, sir! It's not hard to spot people who have the service spirit inside of them. It's not hard at all. It reminds me of the Gatorade ad, "Is it in you?"

Hire employees like the AutoZone folks in Arizona or like the Delta flight attendant. Pay them more if necessary. If you're in the service business, do not tolerate employees who do not have the service spirit in them. It's been my experience that most can't be fixed.

What was the defining difference between the Office Max employee and the AutoZone employees or the difference between the one Delta flight attendant and the other two? It was an internally driven, sincere desire to please the customer—the service spirit—the true definition of customer service.

Now we're going to introduce you to the Circle of Service— a tool kit that can take your business from just being good to a new level of excellence. It's about the service process and involves six relevant areas of attention. They are:

Correlate: Align your service with a clearly defined and understood market niche.

Differentiate: Set your service apart with unique features.

Communicate: Consistently remind your customers why you are their best choice.

Accommodate: Design and deliver service that hits the mark every time.

Regulate: Measure and manage your service.

Innovate: Continuously find new and better ways to serve.

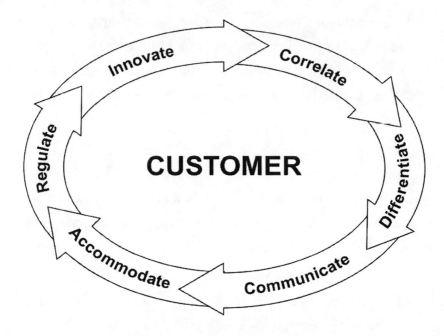

The Circle of Service

This Circle of Service model evolved as a result of our many years of service experience in the retail business. It's a simple method of covering most of the bases in the customer service process and it can be applied by an organization as well as an individual.

The energy that drives the Circle of Service is the energy driven by people who have the service spirit. In other words, by people who have the internally driven, sincere desire to take care of the customer.

Notice the customer is at the center of the circle. Also, notice the graphic illustrates that the six principles form a barrier between your customer and the competition. Think of the old west example of wagons encircling those inside who are being protected.

We also want to emphasize that the circle is not static. It is dynamic, and although the principles don't change, how the principles are applied does change when the market changes.

The Circle of Service can be your business life preserver in a sea of competition.

Let's begin this journey to a higher level of excellence by becoming more familiar with the first principle in the Circle of Service—correlate.

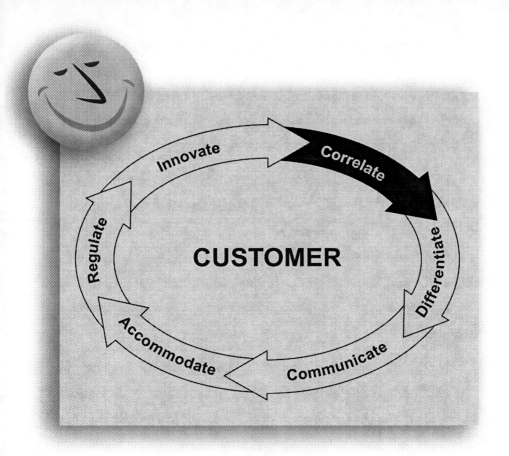

Correlate

To correlate means to align your service with a clearly defined and understood market niche. During the sixties, we owned and operated a fashion shoe store in Boulder, Colorado. We did what we teach! We correlated, or aligned, our service with a specific and clearly defined market niche—the University of Colorado coeds.

Our store was funky, off-beat, and decorated with only coeds in mind. One of our seats was a log from the Colorado Rockies. We cut off the bark on one side and covered it with cushioned purple velvet. Everything was "campy," unusual, and directed at the tastes of affluent college students. People used to come in to the store just to admire the motif.

Our store was located in the heart of the campus on what is referred to as "the hill." Our inventory was stocked with only coeds in mind. Our sales staff was young and savvy. We sold evening shoes that we would tint to match dresses for fraternity parties and formals. We had done a masterful job of correlating our service with the market! The store took off and was a huge success.

Then, with almost no warning, the bottom fell out of our business. Why? The whole fashion scene changed. It was a time of anti-war protesting. The sloppy look became popular and students walked around barefoot or wore only sandals. There was no more evening shoe business. Within a very short period of time we were not correlated with the market at all. Our sales and profits plunged. *Clearly, at this point, we didn't get it!* I know somebody who does get it and he's . . .

Right in Nordstrom's Backyard

Over the years, perhaps you've noticed the demise of fashion specialty shops that are owned and operated by small independents. Any independent who survives in today's environment must precisely correlate and align the business with a well-defined market segment.

A good example of somebody who does is Dale Grant of D. Grant Limited in Salt Lake City, Utah. While other stores have closed, his store has gone on and on. Dale continues to sell $1200 Canali suits, $200 sport shirts, and $300 Zanella slacks. True, this is a limited market, but Dale understands the market and has correlated his business precisely with his target customers. It makes no difference that Nordstom has a big store a block away. Dale's store continues to flourish and win sales awards in the shadows of the giant.

It makes no difference how tough the competition is if you correlate effectively.

Correlation involves the alignment of your service with a clearly defined and understood market niche. Southwest Airlines has done that so well their flight attendants can entertain their passengers with kidding comments such as . . .

Yuck! There's Lipstick on My Glass!

We were on final approach on Southwest Airlines when the flight attendant announced, "Ladies and gentlemen, please wipe the lipstick off your drinking glasses and pass them to the aisle so we can use them on the next flight." The passengers laughed loudly, but I was less amused. Southwest Airlines has done an excellent job aligning its service with a marketing niche of the traveling public. I'm not part of that niche. I avoid Southwest Airlines whenever I can.

I have flown, however, one and a quarter million miles on Delta Airlines. I am usually up front. I like a roomy, assigned seat. I also enjoy the hot, steamy face towels and the formal professionalism of the crew. This does not take away from the fact that Southwest does an excellent job for the part of the public they choose to serve. As for me, I will continue to take my business elsewhere, as long as they correlate with my preferences.

Here are a few ways Delta Airlines correlates with me as part of its target market: The flight attendants have a professional, business-like manner; I have the option of "first class" with warm hand towels, champagne, bigger seats with more room; there is meal service for long flights; seats are assigned to avoid fighting over seats; elite members get a special 800 number for reservations; the flight attendants address their customers in first class by name.

But wait! Things have changed. Delta just filed for bankruptcy. Also, I moved away from a Delta hub and relocated in Phoenix, Arizona. Suddenly Delta was no longer correlated with me. That's why I had to say . . .

Goodbye, Delta—Hello, America West

When I got to Phoenix I decided America West offered more nonstop flights to key cities where I travel. They also fly bigger planes on most of my routes whereas Delta flies regional jets which I hate—too small. America West had all the other stuff too, such as first class seating.

Now, get ready for what happened next! My wife called America West and told them I was a medallion flyer with Delta. She asked if they would give me the same status on the same basis. They did! I was surprised! They have correlated with me very well and so far I've enjoyed their service.

Not only does correlation involve aligning your service with your target consumer's wants, needs, personality, and style, it also involves the alignment of your service with your promises.

> Correlation involves aligning your service with your promises as well as with the customer's wants, needs, personality, and style.
>
> ⊷⊷⊷

Here's an excellent example...of how NOT to do that!

The Plumber's Cracked!

One of the best television ads I ever saw was for an air conditioning and plumbing company. At the end of the commercial, the owner of the company himself, looking into the lens with a smile said, "When you need me, I'll be there."

The problem was, when people needed him, he wasn't there. He went out of business very quickly.

Nothing will turn off customers faster than organizations that don't deliver on promises. Hence, the very trite but true saying, "Under promise and over deliver." You are better off not making a promise if you can't keep it.

Here are some ways Paul the Plumber correlated with his target market: zippo; nada; nothing at all; wasn't there; broken promises; zilch. That was the problem. *Paul the Plumber definitely didn't get it!*

Referring again to our Jamba Juice stores, let me share how we got it and correlated with our market niche.

Jamba Juice really focuses on the daily experience! It is not just about the smoothies. It's about the whole experience and "mystique." In the words of Tom Peters, they believe they should "WOW! each customer every time." Their stores that get it do this by serving only the best quality products and enriching the daily experience of each customer, the community, and themselves through life-nourishing fruits and vegetables.

Always remember, customers are savvy. They are aware of which stores "get it" and which stores don't. In addition, they tell their friends! One customer's experience illustrates this perfectly. Notice the difference from one store to the next. One crew really gets it. The other doesn't (at least on these particular shifts).

I am an avid smoothie drinker. I frequent two of your stores. I love the one in the Arrowhead area. They do an outstanding job. They always greet me upon opening the door and call me by name. Most of the employees even know my smoothie order and have it ready before I pay for it. Everyone is always so

upbeat and energetic. And as far as making me feel important—they do every time.

The other location at Deer Valley is not necessarily bad. They do a good job. But there is a distinct difference in attitude and energy at the other location. For that reason I try to go there whenever possible. Thanks, Jamba! From a loyal Jamba Junkie!"

One Jamba Juice location definitely gets it. They are precisely correlated and aligned with what the customer wants. Here are some ways Jamba Juice correlates with its target niche: Notice how Jamba correlates by focusing on all five of the human senses and overall health:

See: Customers see bright colors, clean buildings, smiling faces and team members in uniform working together.

Hear: Customers hear fun, upbeat music, laughter, greetings, and team members sharing product knowledge.

Smell: Upon entering the store, customers instantly smell a fabulous citrus aroma, not cleaning agents.

Taste: Customers enjoy the best-tasting products made from the freshest ingredients.

Touch: Jamba customers get touched in an emotional way—a real connection with team members.

Health: One of Jamba's goals is to help people live a healthy lifestyle.

Once you have correlated your service approach with your market niche and differentiated yourself from others you automatically create a mystique, an air, an impression about your service.

If your business is not as good as you'd like it to be, start with answering this question:

What is your specific and clearly defined market niche? Describe it in detail. If the answer doesn't flow through your writing instrument with ease, it is likely your business has a correlation problem. That means you need to work on better alignment in the market.

My market niche: _____

_____

_____

_____

_____

_____

_____

_____

_____

_____

_____

Once you align or correlate your service process with a specific market niche, the next step is to apply the second principle of magnetic customer service.

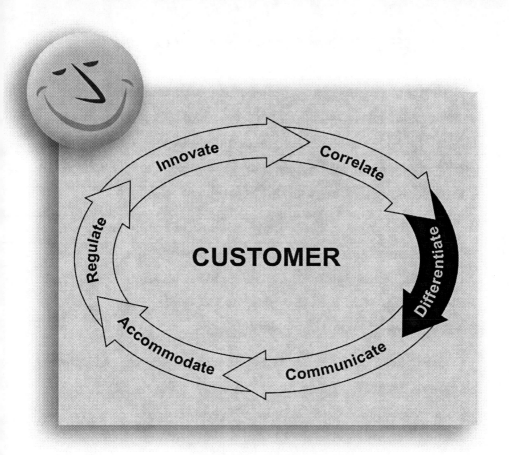

Differentiate

To differentiate means to set your service apart from all the others with unique features.

I live in Phoenix, Arizona. If you have ever been there, you've probably observed a few things. Number one, especially in the middle of summer, you no doubt realized it is about the hottest place on the planet. Number two, it's a huge place. It goes on forever and happens to be one of the fastest-growing cities in America with over four million people already in 2005.

Thirdly, it is retail center heaven. There are more small retail centers here than anywhere I have ever been. There are shops on almost every other corner. It is unbelievable. You can find nearly every brand in America here in Phoenix. As a consumer it's great because there is so much to choose from.

When it comes to food choices alone we have so many, many options in each food category. If you want Asian food you can choose from Tokyo Express, Shogun Express, Oriental Express, Kyoto Bowl, New China Buffet, China Palace, Little Tokyo, Shanghai Club, Bamboo Grill, etc.

For Mexican food, in the "fast food" category alone you have of course, Del Taco, Taco Bell, but also Albertos, Filibertos, Humbertos, Hilibertos, Baja Fresh, Chipoltie, etc.

Get the picture? It's a consumer's paradise, but what about from a seller's perspective?

In today's world, consumers have so many companies to choose from. One of the best things about this great country of ours is free enterprise. But with free enterprise comes competition. And with competition comes the necessity of competing effectively in order to survive.

What is it that sets your company apart? Out of all the companies out there, why would I, as a consumer, choose you and your company? That question is especially obvious when one considers franchised companies, and companies with multiple locations.

Consider a product such as Subway Sandwiches. The sandwiches are the same from location to location. Many franchise owners feel like this is an easy business to get into because of the nationwide branding, commercials, and of course, "Jared." Well, it is fairly easy to open up a Subway Sandwich location or two if you have the money. The challenge is becoming a high volume Subway. The product and brand can only carry you so far. What differentiates the successful stores from the unsuccessful stores is service, or lack thereof. Let me illustrate.

Subway or the Highway?

One evening I went into a Subway location. There were three employees in the shop and not one of them greeted me. As I approached the counter, a young lady came over, put her gloves on and stared at me. I also noticed an older gentleman behind the counter baking cookies. He looked at me with zero acknowledgement. I was so annoyed. I decided to make somebody speak first.

The young lady just stood there looking at me. Up to this point she had done nothing at all. She didn't even smile. I looked back not saying anything either. She, still not saying anything, looked at me with an annoyed expression. I smiled back, hoping to get at least a smile before I spent my hardearned money.

Not able to stand it any longer, she finally said, "Yes? Can I help you?"

I responded with an enthusiastic, "Hello, how are you?"

"Fine," she said in a lackluster manner.

I ordered my sandwich and have not been seen there since. Not many other people have been there either. Wow! What a surprise! *The employees and this particular franchise owner just don't get it!* Fortunately for Subway, they do have many people within their organization who do get it. That's why they are so successful.

It's amazing that such a small thing can make such a big difference. In fact, it's downright incredible—but true that . . .

If you greet all customers within five seconds with a friendly smile you will differentiate your operation from many others.

That's the first step in building . . .

A Well-Oiled Operation

I like one of the ways Auto Maxx entrepreneur, Ralph DeBlasi of Dover, Delaware, differentiates his used car dealership from his competition. Every person who purchases a used car from him gets their oil changed free, on an ongoing basis. He also provides free maintenance evaluations.

Ralph delivers the kind of service in his operation that you'd expect to get in a new car dealership! No wonder he is successful! *Ralph DeBlasi gets it!*

How Sweet It Is!

Splenda, the sweetener, has made a huge dent in the artificial sugar market. It has differentiated itself by positioning itself as the sweetener that tastes like sugar, because it is made from real sugar. It contains no Nutra-Sweet, which people have become very concerned about. This has given Splenda over a 50% market share in the sweetener category in a short period of time.

Can You Spare $5.00 for a Cup of Coffee?

Another example of differentiating is Starbucks Coffee. Starbucks' clientele frequents them for several reasons. Is the coffee really *that* much better than everywhere else? No. It's very good coffee, but most people go there for the atmosphere and the prestige that goes along with Starbucks.

The atmosphere in each Starbucks location defines them. It is a very warm, sophisticated environment. For some reason, a person just feels sophisticated as they enter a Starbucks lobby. But aside from the fine, warm, sophisticated environment and the imported coffee beans from Guatemala and the high hills of Colombia, Starbucks is widely known for their service. As you come to the counter you will receive a "Hi! Welcome to Starbucks. What can I get for you?" delivered with a warm smile!

I have seen a "Now Hiring" sign in their window that is so nice it almost looks like a nice piece of art on the wall. It speaks to the quality of their service. As you look more closely you notice it is a picture of many green apron strings dangling against a nice mocha colored background. It reads:

We're known for our coffee.
But **our people** make us famous!

Join our team. Apply today!
Create the Experience!
Starbucks.com

Starbucks gets it! Make no mistake. They know that their atmosphere and excellent coffee grinds aren't enough to keep people coming back. They have differentiated themselves from the competition. It's the people that *create the experience* and keep them coming back again and again. (Of course, the caffeine addiction helps too.)

There are those restaurants that cater to the sophisticated and those who cater to the less sophisticated. Bobby McGees is a restaurant that is on the other end of the spectrum. It is decorated in a very different way. Not sophisticated, but fun, with loud, upbeat, music playing. The employees are dressed up as different theme characters with a lot of funny expressions on buttons fastened to their suspenders. They cater to a different crowd—the family crowd. Of course one who drinks Starbucks coffee may come here, but it's for a different reason and occasion. It's guaranteed family fun!

It doesn't matter who your target market is, as long as you differentiate your service and correlate with your customer's wants, needs, personality, and desires.

Here are some other *attempts* to differentiate. What has been your experience? Do they?

AVIS	We try harder
McDonald's	We love to see you smile
Baja Fresh	Every order made fresh No microwaves or cans
VISA	We're where you want us to be
Krispy Kreme Donuts	Always hot and fresh
Subway	Bread made fresh daily
Quizno's	Home of the toasted sub

In a Nutshell

Think of your own business. Have you clearly differentiated your service process from the competition? How do you do it?

List the things you do to differentiate your service:

_____

_____

_____

_____

_____

_____

_____

_____

_____

_____

_____

_____

_____

_____

_____

_____

Differentiate is the second principle of magnetic service. It makes your operation stand out! It will get word-of-mouth advertising going, but it's still vital to apply the third principle in the Circle of Service . . .

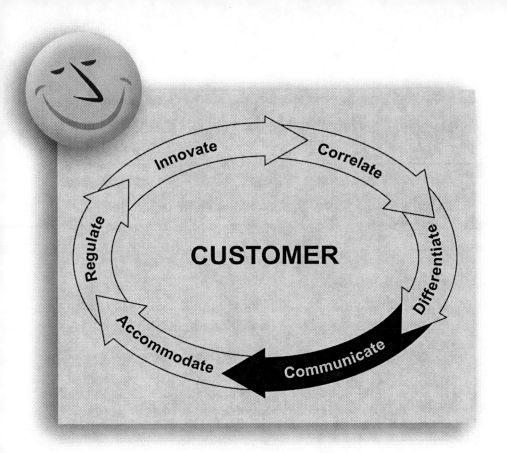

Communicate

Communication in magnetic customer service means—To consistently remind your customers why you are their best choice!

The Dumb Dentist?

One day when I was very young, I went to the dentist for a checkup. His name was Dr. Brough, a jovial, round man with a mustache. As he examined my teeth he kept commenting on the incredible, beautiful, dental work I had in my mouth. Then he said, "Who did it?"

When I got home I told my dad that Doc Brough was really dumb. He didn't even remember he was the dentist who did the previous work.

Dad laughed and said, "Oh, yes he did. He says that to all of his patients. He doesn't want anybody to forget how good he really is!"

That's one example of the third element of service in action – Communicate!

> ## You need to constantly remind your customers why you are their best choice.

How do companies who get it, do that? One way is with an effective slogan. Their slogan is repeated over and over again, in print advertising, on radio and television commercials, on their website, and in-store advertising. If we were to mention some companies, their slogan would probably jump into your mind. Here are three examples:

Allstate: "You're in good hands with Allstate."

Alta Ski Resort: "Alta is for Skiers."

Southwest Airlines: "You are now free to move about the country."

Notice that the slogan often invokes two things. First, it's a reminder that they cater to a target niche. For example, the slogan Southwest Airlines uses, "You are now free to move about the country," is directed at the economy market.

Secondly, it's a statement of differentiation. Remember Quizno's slogan? "It's toasty here." That one simple element of differentiation is forcing Subway to toast their sandwiches too! This is an excellent reminder that differentiation is never static.

Here's how Southwest Airlines reminds customers they are the best deal in their market. When it's snack time they pass out a little bag of peanuts in metallic blue wrapping with copper edges. They have a picture of an airplane on the packet with their Internet web address. It's very attractive! But in the center of that blue package in white lettering is the word "Byte-sized Fares." Think of it! Everybody on the airplane gets the packet of peanuts and is reminded again that Southwest Airlines has low fares.

You must constantly create new and unique ways to differentiate and communicate. Communication boils down to this— it doesn't matter what you do well, if people don't know you do it. Tell them! And remind them constantly! A good example of this is how…

In-N-Out Gets the Word Out

When we are in California we like to buy burgers at In-N-Out. They have a very clever way of communicating why their French fries are better. Printed in the bottom of every cardboard French fry holder is this statement:

"Since 1948 we've been cooking our fries in 100% cholesterol-free vegetable oil. Our potatoes are peeled and diced at each store and cooked fresh for you." In-N-Out Burger

This happens to be just one of the reasons we eat there and avoid McDonald's. When it comes to communication, *In-N-Out Burger gets it.*

Speaking of burgers, have you ever heard of . . .

Ketchup for Trekkies?

Here's a new and unique way Heinz is reminding customers that their ketchup is still the best choice. This is on the back of the ketchup bottle in my refrigerator:

For a limited time, some of your favorite stars are telling the world why they love the thick and rich taste of Heinz Ketchup. And Heinz is saying thank you by donating to the charities of their choice.

And this is on the front of that ketchup bottle:

"Fixes burgers at warp speed."

~ William Shatner ~

Heinz has been in business since 1869. *Heinz definitely gets it!*

I always thought the old Burger King slogan was a good one, "Have it your way." How many places do you go to today where there are no substitutions? Which reminds me—in a negative way—of the following story told to me by one of my friends.

Don't Hire an Egghead!

We went to breakfast at a restaurant where the senior special was two eggs, bacon, hash browns, and toast for $1.99.

"Sounds good," my wife said. "But I don't want the eggs."

"Then I'll have to charge you $2.49 because you're ordering a la carte," the waitress warned her.

"You mean, I'll have to pay for not taking the eggs?" my wife asked incredulously and then finished with, "I'll take the special."

"How do you want your eggs?" asked the waitress.

"Raw and in the shell," my wife replied.

She took the two eggs home.* *That restaurant didn't get it!*

They especially don't know that communication is . . .

More than Words

Often when we think of communication we think of what we direct to consumers in print and electronic media. But wait, communication experts tell us that everything that happens in a relationship is communication—Everything!

Let's pull this together . . .

We've said the third element of a superior customer service process is communicate. That means to constantly remind your customers why you are their best choice.

Everything you do should communicate that. Here's what I mean when I say everything! It happened the night . . .

There Was a Nut Working at
Grovestand Snacks in Vegas!

It was a scratchy contact lens night. I had been working hard all day and landed at Las Vegas late in the evening to switch planes. I was hungry and as I neared the top of the escalator I saw a sign that read, "Grovestand." Perfect! I didn't have time for a meal. There was the server sitting in a chair with her feet up on a stool reading a paperback novel. Clearly she was hoping she wouldn't have to speak to any customers.

"I'd like some cashews," I said.

Not moving, still sitting, leaning back in the chair with her feet propped up and trying to talk me out of a purchase, she said, "That'll probably cost you at least six bucks!"

There was no way I would leave without making her get out of the chair.

Every time I see a Grovestand, I remember that incident. The reason? Customers remember shoddy service. They remember very, very well.

The communication sent was easy to understand. "Don't bother me! I don't want to help any customers this evening!"

Here are some other examples of how everything that happens is communication.

- **Communication sent!** I had lunch at Piñata Nueva in Anthem, Arizona. The hostess escorted me to a seat, tossed a menu on the table with her back to me, and walked away.

Message received? "You're not special!" *Piñata Nueva doesn't get it!*

- **Communication sent!** I drove by a pizza shop in a strange town. There was a large sign in the window that said, "Free smells."

Message received? "We are different, fun, and you'll be served on the relationship channel." *This pizza shop gets it!*

- **Communication sent!** My son took me to a restaurant that has great food, Carlos O'Brien's in Phoenix, Arizona. I loved the food and the service. Then I went into their dirty bathroom.

Message received? "Our kitchen is dirty too." I drove by there the other day. That location is out of business. *They didn't get it!*

- **Communication sent!** I went to Safeway and bought $24.00 worth of groceries. The checker smiled, used my name and said, "Thanks, Mr. Woods, you saved $3.50 today. Would you like help out with that?"

Message received? "We have great values here and we appreciate our customers." Every time I visit Safeway I get similar treatment. *Safeway gets it!*

- **Communication sent!** My wife told the store manager at Fry's grocery store she wanted to return a patio umbrella that didn't function properly. Every time she made a statement, the manager's response was curt, clippie, and caustic.

Message received? "You're a pain in the butt and I don't trust what you are saying." *This manager doesn't get it!*

- **Communication sent!** My wife tried a new dry cleaner and just brought the cleaning home. And there it was, a communication idea I had never seen before. Stapled to the plastic bag, covering my shirts, was a real picture of Brian O'Neil, a real estate agent, reminding me why he should be my first choice in real estate. Very revolutionary!

Message received? "I am your best choice when you are ready." *Brian O'Neil gets it!*

Again . . .

> It doesn't matter what you do if people don't know you do it, so be sure to tell them and remind them continually.

And remember, communication is not limited to what you say or how you say it. It includes everything you do including making it easy for your customers to give you feedback.

Keep telling customers why you are good, and make it easy for them to validate that with feedback. It's likely when you are in a service establishment and you don't like the service, there will probably not be an evaluation form handy. Hmmmm! There must be a connection here! I find when establishments make it easy to give feedback, the service is always better.

I think the best feedback form I ever saw was in a pizza joint in Boston. It simply said, "Was your experience good enough that you'd recommend us to a friend? If not, why?" That was it. No long lists of questions, no boxes to check, just one simple question.

We need to remember the customer's perception is controlled by a mental picture of what they want. This mental picture consists of a set of imagined expectations that make up the total customer experience they are seeking.

Your service performance is tested against the service expectations in the customer's mind. Every time you serve a customer, you are automatically evaluated on their mental computer. Your score computes to either expectations met or expectations not met. Through this process the customer concludes whether he or she will or will not choose to return to you again.

The person's mental software, testing whether or not you meet his or her expectations, usually operates in the twelve general areas of service values. These values have been isolated through years of experience in customer service. They are:

Prompt recognition – The first signal your service will be excellent.

Friendliness – People are quickly satisfied in a friendly environment.

Rapport – Making a connection on the relationship channel.

Competency – People want to deal with an expert.

Speed – Customers want you to hurry, even if they want to take their time.

Simplicity – Nobody wants complex or complicated transactions.

Value – All customers look for this. It's a major consideration.

Integrity – The glue that will get customers to stick with you.

Cleanliness – People shun physical space that is not well maintained.

Appreciation – Customers like to be told they are appreciated.

Memory – This means don't forget who they are, their names, and preferences.

Prompt Follow-up – Customers want you to follow-up promptly when they request something.

Furthermore, customers will use all of their senses in the evaluation process—what they see, what they smell, what they hear, and what they feel. Customers stop doing business with firms that don't measure up, or firms that don't get it. Make it easy for them to communicate to you how they feel about what you are communicating to them.

List the ways you communicate to your customers that you are their best choice:

_____

_____

_____

_____

_____

_____

_____

_____

_____

_____

_____

_____

_____

We are talking about the six elements in the Circle of Service. We've discussed the first three. They are: Correlate, Differentiate, and Communicate. Now let's talk about the fourth element of the customer service process.

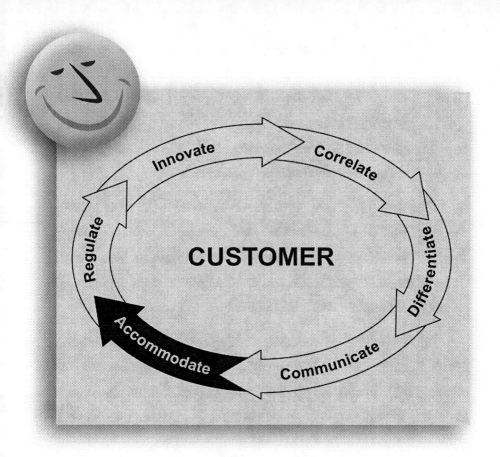

Accommodate

To accommodate means to design and follow a customer service delivery process that hits the mark every time! There are three keys to accommodating customers in the most effective way. They are:

1. Design, write, and follow a service plan.

2. Promote a happy environment.

3. Become personally empowered and build an empowered team.

Let's begin with the process of delivering your service based upon a pre-determined, written service plan. In other words, you can't provide service excellence until you first design the process for accommodating the customer.

If I were consulting with your company, the first thing I would ask to see is your written service plan. Do you have one? You would never build a house without a blueprint. You would first design it. If you really want to achieve customer service excellence it must first be designed.

The purpose of a business is to create and keep customers. And because a quality service process keeps customers coming back, quality service is critical to your success! In fact, service is the most vital element of your success. It's the very reason for your existence as a business.

Since customer service is the key, let's see if we can understand it more completely. The objective of the service process is consistently accommodating clientele in a way that meets or exceeds their wants.

The starting point in understanding the service process is to think of it as a commodity. It's a commodity like any product sold, and has value. But even though it is a commodity of value, it often doesn't get the attention it deserves—possibly in part because of these unique features:

- It is intangible.

- It is created and consumed at the same time.

- It is a total experience created by a set of individual experiences.

- It is human-being intensive.

- Whether it happens or doesn't depends upon what the customer thinks.

- It is both emotional and physical.

- It cannot be stored like merchandise.

Clearly because of the intangible nature of service, our first challenge in designing a service plan is to make it more tangible so that those who actually perform the service know what experience they are to create to fulfill the customer's expectations.

How Is This Accomplished?

The same way customers do it—they **describe the service.** Have you noticed when somebody tells you about excellent service they describe the events they enjoyed about the service?

Service design is a written description of the events you will orchestrate to create the total service experience—from start to finish. This description is in the form of a series of service goals. A service goal is an event you seek to create for, or on behalf of, the customer.

A service goal is a predetermined activity or event. Simply list each activity you want your customer to experience as you accommodate them and cater to their requests. An activity is something you do. Activities are the basic building blocks of customer service design. Simply lay out in written sequence each activity you want to engage in as you move your customer through the accommodating process. From the time you greet the customer (an activity/event) to the time you thank them and say good-bye (an activity/event).

Here is a quick look at a sampling of the customer design format we used in our retail shoe stores.

There was a great retail era years ago, prior to the big chains. Each city had its own set of exclusive independent merchants. Stores had their own personalities and unique merchandise. Everything wasn't "the same." It was fun to shop and discover, and, in my opinion, service was better.

Here is a quick look at the outline of our customer service plan, the one we used in our exclusive retail shoe stores during the golden years of retailing. We called our plan . . .

The Ten Steps to Sales and Service

Step 1:   Greet and Seat the Customer

Step 2:   Remove the Customer's Shoe

Step 3:   Decide What to Show the Customer

Step 4:   Show the Customer the Shoes

Step 5:   Tell the Customer About the Shoes

Step 6:   Narrow the Selection

Step 7:   Resolve Objections

Step 8:   Close the Sale

Step 9:   Show and Sell Additional Pairs of Shoes

Step 10:   Establish After-Sales Rapport

Whenever new employees are trained, it is explained that great customer service means different things to different people.

After outlining the steps of our shoe selling service we then designed in written form what we wanted the customer to experience in each of the ten steps. The details included such things as the correct way to smile, how to welcome the customer, the correct posture for sitting on the fitting stool, how to show shoes and how to enhance rapport after the sale.

The net effect was simply this, customers felt as though they were a special guest in our home rather than just any old customer.

If you'll design your service process in written form and train your staff to follow it, you'll be amazed at the quality of your service process. More importantly, your customers will too!

Glass Half Full or Glass Half Empty?

Some of our best opportunities to shine come in handling problems. It is also crucial, as part of your plan, to design activities for recovering from customer complaints. Complaints will occur no matter how sharp your organization is, so be prepared for something along the lines of . . .

Who Moved My Salad?

I was dining with a friend in a new, very nice restaurant in Boise, Idaho, some years ago. Determined to eat fairly light, I ordered a chef salad. Soon the server appeared with one of the most beautiful sculptures in lettuce and vegetables I'd ever seen. I poised my fork to partake of the first taste when suddenly the salad moved. There, on top of the salad, was a large grasshopper about two inches in length.

I called the server back and remarked, "I didn't order a grasshopper salad. I ordered a chef salad. I said it in a fun way, but I did complain. I was entitled to do so.

Clearly they hadn't designed a service recovery plan. They offered nothing but a terse, "I'm sorry," and as far as I'm concerned, they bumbled the whole incident. It reminded me of the old joke, "Oh, waiter! There's a fly in my soup!" To which the waiter replies, "Don't worry! He won't eat much!"

I frequently dine out and often the server will come back and ask, "How is everything?" (part of the service plan, no doubt). Sometimes when I do mention something isn't just right, I do get a blank stare!?!

Resolving complaints really isn't difficult. There are basically two methods: 1) The Quick Fix, and 2) The Collaborative Method.

The Quick Fix Solution

The quick fix is when the cause of the problem is strictly your fault and the remedy is obvious…such as a grasshopper in the salad. The intent here is to overwhelm the customer with your desire to please and the promptness with which it is done. The quick fix should be fun and impressive.

The Collaborative Solution

The collaborative solution is used when you rely on the customer to assist you in determining what sort of adjustment would be fair. You'll discover that the customer often asks for less than you would be willing to give.

The technique in using the collaborative solution involves two approaches. One way is to suggest options to the customer and let them choose what they feel would be a fair fix. The other is to get the customer to suggest to you what they feel would resolve the problem fairly. Then, do it!

The objective in resolving a complaint or problem is to make the customer happy again! And to do it without giving away the store!

Happy Customers Come Back!
Sign in Hardees Training Room
Baltimore, Maryland

There are five service recovery building blocks that can be used to make the customer happy again. These should always be used when using the quick fix or the collaborative solution.

1. **Listen:** Listen carefully and patiently to the problem.

2. **Apologize:** Customers expect an apology. Use the endangered species words, "I'm sorry!"

3. **Reassure:** Let the customer know the problem will be properly resolved.

4. **Resolve the problem:** Depending on the circumstance, use the quick fix or the collaborative solution.

5. **Be grateful:** Thank the customer for bringing the problem to your attention. Thank goodness for customers who complain to you instead of to their friends at work, at the health club, or wherever they go!

In service recovery, the thanks should be verbal or written, plus "something extra" in appreciation for the time they took to tell you about the problem. The "something extra" also compensates them for the inconvenience.

Here's how Yoplait did it when my daughter found a hair in her yogurt.

They Don't Yoplait Around!

Dear Ms. Woods:

Thank you for contacting us. We know it would be disturbing to find hair in a food and we are sorry you had this unpleasant experience with Yoplait Light strawberry yogurt.

Great care is taken to prevent this from happening. All employees are required to wear head coverings while in production areas of the plant.

You are right to expect high-quality products, and we appreciate your telling us about this matter. The information you have given us will be carefully reviewed with the people who work with this product.

Enclosed is a refund for your purchase along with gift coupons which we hope you will enjoy.

Sincerely,

Jan Ecklund

Yoplait gets it!

Yes, designing, writing, and following a service plan is the first key to accommodating the customer effectively.

Now let's talk about the second key—Promote a Happy Environment.

A positive environment is the fresh air and water of service excellence. Nourishment for a positive, happy, service environment starts from the top! I was especially aware of this the day I heard somebody say . . .

Ding! Dong! The Witch Is Dead!

A happy service environment begins with leadership. When frontline employees are not upbeat and friendly to consumers, it is symptomatic of ineffective leadership.

I worked in a very fine specialty store chain in my career. Morale was very low. The climate reminded me of a poster that hangs tongue-in-cheek in my friend's office. Written below a skull-and-crossbones is this slogan: "Beatings will continue until morale improves."

Everybody knew who the problem was. One day this person quit and I got a telephone call from a fellow employee who called and said, "Ding! Dong! The witch is dead!" From that point on, beatings ended and morale began to improve.

There is no room for the slightest degree of negativism in a service establishment. Remember, the true definition of customer service is, "an internally driven sincere desire to take care of the customer." Negativism is a cancer that can get in the way of fulfilling that objective.

"If you want your customers to receive the finest service in the world, treat your employees exactly the way you want your customers treated."

Tom Peters

The third key to accommodating the customer in the most effective way is to become personally empowered and build an empowered team.

Do yourself a favor and read what I think is the best book out there on the subject. It was written by William A. Guillory, Ph.D., and is entitled, *Empowerment for High Performing Organizations.*

Let's begin by making references to Guillory's definitions.

Empower: To empower means to have the ability and be granted the authority to carry out one's, or a team's, responsibilities within mutually agreed upon guidelines between a supervisor and an individual or a team.

Empowerment: the capacity of an individual, a team, or an organization to perform at or above the level of a customer's expectations. It is based upon two concepts: 1) personal responsibility, and 2) personal accountability.

When service providers are not empowered, very often, the customer is not accommodated effectively. That's why one evening I got really . . .

Cheesy Service

I flew into St. Louis at the end of a tough day. It was late. I was hungry and pleased to see pizza as the house specialty at my hotel.

They had two choices—pepperoni or three-cheese pizza. I love cheese, so I ordered a three-cheese pizza and a small coke.

It took a long time, but finally the server showed up at my door, dropped the order on the table in my room, wheeled around, handed me the check to sign and was out of there. Only

SERVICE! Some People Just Don't Get It!

then did I discover that she had delivered not one, but three huge, three-cheese pizzas.

Clearly, something was very wrong with this picture. One man . . . in a small room . . . with one small coke . . . and three giant pizzas!

An empowered employee would have observed the problem. Not this server! Her job was to just deliver the food. That's all!

An empowered employee would have taken personal responsibility to ensure my satisfaction.

You probably have many examples of your own when things went awry because the service provider was not empowered. It was that very reason I got . . .

Hung Up at Red Hanger Cleaners

I was in the process of re-hanging our draperies after picking them up from a Red Hanger Cleaners location. Whoops! They weren't properly pressed.

I immediately returned them and explained the problem. The counter person just looked at me with a blank stare and said, "You'll have to see the manager."

To which I replied, "Okay. Let me speak to the manager."

Another blank stare accompanied the comment, "The manager isn't in."

To which I replied, "When will the manager be in?"

A third blank stare, "I don't know!" There was a subliminal message here, "And what's more, I don't care! It's not my problem!"

No empowerment! I think the dumbest words in customer service are: "You'll have to talk to the manager." I hope they aren't used in your organization.

By that I don't mean help shouldn't be solicited from management when an adjustment is very difficult. What I mean is that the words, "You'll have to talk to . . . " are a complete turn-off and shouldn't be used in any customer interaction.

In a Nutshell

Accommodate is the fourth principle in the Circle of Service. Accommodate means to design and follow a customer service process that hits the mark every time.

There are three key areas to ensure this happens:

1. Design, write, and follow a service plan.

2. Promote a happy environment.

3. Become personally empowered and build an empowered team.

How about your organization? We invite you to answer the following questions.

1. Do you have a service plan in writing, including a pre-arranged plan for dealing with complaints?

   _____

   _____

   _____

2. Is your service plan followed?

   _____

   _____

   _____

3. How is morale? What do you do to promote a happy environment?

   _____

   _____

   _____

4. Are you and your team personally empowered to perform at or above the level of a customer's expectation?

   _____

   _____

   _____

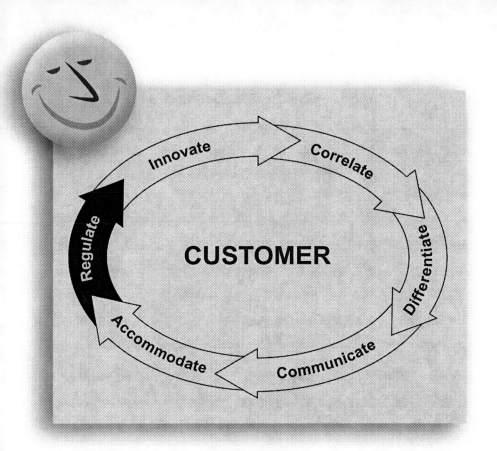

Regulate

Regulate is the fifth element in the Circle of Service. It means—To measure and manage your service process. It involves:

- Measuring your service performance against your service plan.

- Controlling the service sinkers.

- Training everybody in the organization to enrich the service process with the six service savers.

- Using a time management tool to track and keep promises.

High-Flying Customer Service
or
The Service Was Sooooooo Good that I Married the Flight Attendant

As part of the process of writing this book I decided I would evaluate the service on three major airlines. I thought it would be a fun thing to do since I fly so much. I selected American, United and Delta. I made up a little checklist to evaluate the service I received from the first contact with the gate agent to the last thing that was said to me when I got off the plane.

One morning I boarded a United flight and was blown away by their customer service excellence. Really! It was extraordinary. It was the second best service I've ever received on an airline.

I say the second-best because the best was a United flight on which I met and then later married the flight attendant. But that's another story, the details of which are found in the book *Tick Tock Who Broke the Clock?* by William A. Guillory and myself.

So, back to the story. On this particular morning I noticed that every flight attendant was well groomed (they didn't look like they had just climbed out of bed) and they smiled. They smiled at everybody.

When the captain gave his announcement he was so good I was convinced he quite possibly might be the best pilot in the sky. It was very reassuring. What a sales job he did! I continued to watch this customer service excellence unfold before my very eyes.

Time for food service. Flight attendants went out of their way to personalize their interaction with each passenger (the relationship channel). After completion of the food service they rang the intercom bell and made this announcement, "Ladies and gentlemen, we're going to be coming through the aircraft passing out a form to evaluate the service on this flight." I smiled and thought of several old axioms:

"Measurement motivates."

And, "Where performance is measured, performance improves."

And also, "Where performance is measured and reported back, performance accelerates!"

Actually I was a little disappointed because I thought the excellence of this crew was the result of their sheer professionalism. To a large degree they were, but there is no question—measurement motivates.

It's easy to measure service in an airline because they have a pre-determined service plan that the crew is expected to follow from start to finish, (i.e., greeting and seating, safety announcement, drink service, food service, landing preparation, etc.). One need only ask two questions: 1) Was the format followed? and 2) On a scale of 1-10, how effective were they on the transaction and relationship channels?

In your own business, if you haven't taken the time to design a service plan from start to finish you'll have nothing to measure. If you do have a service plan then you have something to measure and you are ready to implement the sixth principle of service excellence—Regulate!

> Regulate means to consistently measure your service performance against your service plan.
>
> +>==—=<+

The toenail experience is an example of one hotel that gets it by regulating their service and how the other hotel doesn't get it.

Ugh! Somebody's Toenails Are Under My Bed!

I flew into Portland one night and checked into a hotel only to find the room wasn't very clean. It was very late and I was tired so I decided to stay there anyway.

As I was unpacking, I dropped my manicure scissors and they fell under the bed. I got down on my knees to retrieve them. I looked under my bed. (I don't recommend this.) It was dirty, but even worse, what I saw under my bed was a little pile of somebody's toenails. I never went back to that hotel again.

A couple of months later I was traveling in the Northeast and checked into a Marriott Hotel near Boston. Strangely enough, I dropped something and had to look under the bed to retrieve it (not an exciting prospect after my last under-the-bed experience in the previous hotel). It was immaculate under there.

The only thing under the bed was a little tent sign which read, "Yes! We look here too!" And it was initialed by every person who cleaned the room that week. Impressive! How does that happen?

It happens because the principle of regulation is being used. First, a written plan, and then, consistently measuring performance against that plan.

Another way to regulate your service is by paying particular attention to an important key we've already mentioned—Create a happy environment. Surround yourself with positive people. That certainly wasn't happening in the company where I saw . .

The Efficient Grouch

I was observing the cashier while standing in the food line at a very prestigious pharmaceutical company. She was a grouchy middle-aged woman who didn't smile and snapped at customers like a hungry piranha fish. She reminded me of the Soup Nazi on the Seinfeld Show.

I turned to an executive standing next to me and asked, "What's with her?"

"Oh!" he said. "She's a real grouch, but she's so efficient nobody wants to let her go."

They just don't get it! There is no room in a service organization for a grouch who operates only on the transaction channel. If you have such a person, help get them relocated ASAP! Clearly such a person does not have the service spirit, that internally driven, sincere desire to take care of the customer.

Employees who don't have the service spirit can slowly erode your clientele in subtle ways. Or they can automatically damage your reputation. Such an example appeared on television news last night.

An agent for a well-known telecommunication company addressed a letter to a disgruntled customer starting with, "Dear Bitch." He, of course, was fired, but it did make national news. Who needs that kind of advertising?

To regulate also involves recognizing and eliminating what we call the service sinkers. Service sinkers can be self-imposed or system-imposed if we are operating as part of a service team.

Following are two service sinker lists. I invite you to take a few minutes and evaluate your performance individually and as a team. Put a check by those that impact you or your organization the most.

System-Imposed Service Sinkers

_____ Service not measured

_____ Don't hold service meetings

_____ Improper delegation

_____ Understaffing

_____ No vision statement

_____ No prearranged complaint response

_____ Measure the wrong things

_____ No service design

_____ High employee turnover

_____ Careless hiring

_____ Lack of simplification

_____ Don't keep track of who your customers are

_____ Negative policies

_____ Failure to articulate service values and objectives

_____ Lack of generosity in resolving complaints

_____ Lack of authority given to service person

_____ Management not in touch with front-line personnel

_____ Lack of mission statement

_____ Tolerating the "efficient grouch"

_____ Service goals unclear

_____ Ineffective communication

_____ Avoid rewards and recognition

_____ Break promises

_____ Lack of management commitment

_____ Unwilling to pay the price

_____ Shortsightedness

_____ Inattention to details

_____ Ignore feedback

_____ Fail to make service everybody's job

_____ Overstaffing

_____ Fear of making needed changes

_____ Mixed signals from management

_____ Failure to praise service success and effort

_____ Don't customize

_____ Over-regulate service people with rules and
procedures

_____ Make it difficult for customers to complain

_____ Failure to treat employees like customers

_____ Gap between service promise and service
delivery

_____ Lack of service standards

_____ Failure to clarify what's expected

_____ Making excuses

_____ No training program

List your three most serious system-imposed service sinkers below:

1. _____

2. _____

3. _____

Self-Imposed Service Sinkers

_____ Poor time management

_____ Move slowly

_____ Poor records

_____ Can't remember names

_____ Work too long

_____ Don't take breaks

_____ Preoccupation

_____ Lack of knowledge

_____ Overtired

_____ Negative, nonverbal communication

_____ Avoid eye contact

_____ Lack of commitment

_____ Treat customers as interruptions

_____ Lack of follow-up

_____ Lack of enthusiasm

_____ Ignore customers

_____ Excessive chitchat with employees

_____ Over-visiting with the customer

_____ Failure to put the customer first

_____ Lack of follow-through

_____ Stringing customers along

_____ Vague answers

_____ Ignore details

_____ No personal service standards

_____ Lack of personal organization

_____ Not listening

_____ Making excuses

_____ Poor personal hygiene

_____ Don't customize

_____ Don't remember customers

_____ Unfamiliar with procedures

_____ Unfamiliar with technology

_____ Putting the telephone customer ahead of the

in-person customer

_____ Dishonesty with the customer

_____ Don't measure service

_____ Lack of mission statement

_____ Negative attitude

List your three most serious self-imposed service sinkers below:

1. _____

2. _____

3. _____

You can't fix all of the service sinkers in your organization at once. Start with one of the three most serious you've identified and then move on to another.

The third element of regulate is train, train, and train. Train each member of your team to enrich every transaction and relationship with . . .

The Six Service Savers

Service Saver 1 – <u>Connect!</u> Connect with the customer first before anything else. Welcome all customers as though they are guests in your home. Not this way: I walked into a private club at a ski resort and sat down. The bartender shouted at me across the room in a very unfriendly tone, "Ya have a membership?" **Message sent:** Don't get too comfortable! **Message received:** Buddy, I'm not sure you are welcome here.

Service Saver 2 – <u>Clarify!</u> When you think you understand what the customer wants, repeat it back to him/her. That way this won't happen: While attempting to have a nice breakfast one morning I ordered ala carte and told the server I wanted two eggs over easy and a side of bacon. She said "OK." When she brought my food it was one egg and a side of bacon. **Message sent:** I really don't care enough to get it right. **Message received:** This is not a good place to have breakfast.

Service Saver 3 – <u>Comply!</u> When complying with a customer request it is vital to respond quickly. Customers want you to hurry even though they want to take their time. The best job I ever saw with this was in a restaurant where they guarantee your lunch will be served in 15 minutes or it's free. After taking the order the server puts a stopwatch on the table and punches in the time. WOW! **Message sent:** We mean what we say! **Message received:** We keep our promises! And they did. As you might expect, the restaurant was jammed.

Service Saver 4 – <u>Customize!</u> When customizing, you walk the path of the customer's style—monochronic or polychronic (as described on pages 8-9). You also adapt to special requests.

Customers expect and want a degree of flexibility. Be willing to adjust to individual styles and requests. Not like this: My spouse and I often like to split meals since portions are so large today. We were trying out a new restaurant and the server said we couldn't split a meal. Why? The chef doesn't like to do it. **Message sent:** We don't really care what you want. **Message received:** We don't go out of our way for customers. Consequently we won't go out of our way to go back because we certainly wouldn't want to inconvenience the chef.

When customizing, you cater to special customer requests without letting it throw you. And it's done with a S<u>M</u>ILE as opposed to a S<u>N</u>ILE (Snile: facial muscles up without sincerity).

Service Saver 5 – <u>Consistency!</u> Consistency is crucial. When a service establishment is not consistent with service delivery, customers feel like they are being jerked back and forth like the tip of a fly rod. One expert put it this way, "Consistency is so important, if you're going to serve a bad cup of coffee, make sure you always serve a bad cup of coffee." When going from one location in a chain operation to another we all expect consistency, but unfortunately that isn't always the case.

Had my sport coat alteration experience been enriched with service saver 5, I would not have said on a particular day . . .

The Men's Wearhouse Isn't My House

We bought a sport coat in The Men's Wearhouse in Salt Lake City and we were pleased with the service but, because of my schedule, I had to get it altered in another state.

I was excited when I walked into the store to get my coat altered because I was planning on buying some ties and maybe some shirts to go with my new coat.

My excitement ended when I was greeted with, "Ya buy that here?" "No." "We have to charge for alterations. Go stand over by that mirror and I'll go get the tailor." My whole experience was in that tone. I couldn't wait to get out of there. I was treated as though I was an intrusion. Every one of the six service savers was missing including service saver 5--Consistency. I expected I would get the same fine service as the Salt Lake store but I didn't.

On my way out I saw many ties that would have gone with my sport coat, but of course I didn't buy and I never will at that location.

Service Saver 6 – <u>Conclude!</u> This is a critical element of service success. How you conclude will be the last thing on the customer's mind. This service saver has six parts:

1. Verify satisfaction.

2. Genuinely thank the customer.

3. Make a statement of appreciation.

4. Reassure the customer about their decision.

5. Invite them back.

6. Use the customer's name.

Sound complicated? It's not really! Emphasize these six steps as a habit and it will lift up the quality of your service.

Had McDonald's enriched the following service experience with service saver 6 my spouse would not have been so irritated the day she was served . . .

A Barbecued Milkshake

A few months ago my wife purchased a chocolate milkshake, among other things, at McDonald's. Upon the first sip, after getting all the way home, she noticed it tasted like barbecue sauce. "What in the world?" she thought. It was absolutely disgusting. So she got all four kids back into the car (not an easy task in 105 degree weather in the middle of an Arizona summer) and they went back to the "golden arches."

When she explained her plight to the young teen at the register, another employee said very audibly, "Oh! She got it."

My wife said, "What do you mean?"

"Well," the employee continued, "someone accidentally hooked up the barbecue pump to the shake machine instead of the chocolate. They look the same. We'll get you another one."

No apology. Only snickers and giggles, as if it wasn't a big deal. As one of them was filling the shake, my wife said, "Do you realize what a hassle it was for me to get all my kids back into the car once home and come all the way over here?"

That was received with only a shoulder shrug; still no apology. She continued with, "So what are you going to do for me?" (Note: had the employees acted the least bit apologetic she wouldn't have made a big deal out of it because mistakes happen.) He then handed her a small bag of fries, still without an apology.

Before we get off the subject of training, we highly recommend some meeting time is set aside exclusively for customer service training. No other subject should be discussed at those meetings. They should be short, about 15 minutes on average. They should also be positive and function like a business pep rally. Here is a suggested agenda:

Service Meeting Outline

I.   A success story

II. One service problem and suggested solutions

III. Service training topic: Transaction Channel

IV. Service training topic: Relationship Channel

V.   Employee recognition

Short but frequent meetings are the best way to go. This will keep service in the forefront and visible in your organization.

Conclusion and Summary

The fifth principle in the Circle of Service is regulate. Regulating involves continuously measuring your service process performance against your written service plan, controlling service sinkers, and training everyone within the organization to enrich the service process with the six service savers.

Another component of regulate is to use a time management tool effectively to track and keep promises.

Promise keeping is crucial to superior customer service. Promises and commitments are often broken because service providers don't have a system to track commitments. Knowing how to use a good self-management tool such as a Day-Timer® can insure nothing will fall through the cracks.

I like pocket-size organizers in the customer service field because they are small, portable and convenient. I also prefer paper planners to electronic because in a service setting they are faster. The key is to select the size that you are willing to take with you wherever you go. That's vital! If you have it with you to document service commitments, dates and deadlines you'll always be able to keep your promises.

Here's how to use a self-management tool to maximize results. Make sure the tool you select has a set of twelve monthly calendars for the entire year; a daily appointments and planning space; a space for documenting vital information; and a catch-all list space.

Let's talk for a moment about how to use each of these areas to your greatest advantage.

We'll begin with the monthly calendar. The monthly calendar is a like a master control panel. Use it for all of your appointments, dates, deadlines and follow-up times. Keep it current and updated so you can depend upon it.

Use the dated daily pages for two things. First, it is a place to build a daily plan which includes a simple action list as well as your appointment schedule. Second, use your daily pages for documenting information that comes to you during the day through your customer interactions. This is where you document promises to customers. Anytime you write down an item that needs follow-up, place an asterisk (*) by that item. This will get your attention and remind you to follow up.

I cannot stress enough how crucial it is for customer service agents to use the daily journal or documenting pages rather than writing vital information on bits and pieces of paper that are loose. Little pieces of paper with important information get lost, and this often creates a customer service breakdown.

To further avoid using bits and pieces of paper, set up a catch-all space in your time management tool. Use it for reminders to yourself or to build a master task list of things you need to follow-up on.

In a Nutshell

When you regulate you simply make sure everyone and everything in your organization is meeting the standards your customers have helped you identify as being important to them.

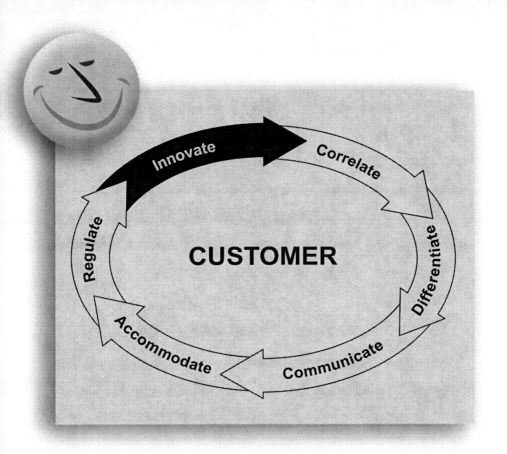

Innovate

To innovate means to continuously find new and better ways to serve. Managing a customer service process is not static. It is dynamic.

When you innovate effectively, the competition will ultimately copy you and intensify competitiveness. Therefore, you will be required to innovate again and again. The rule is: Innovate or Die. A positive outcome is that innovative competition benefits the consumer. I've seen the following quote by a famous retailer validated again and again.

> ## "As competition increases service improves."
>
> ### *Stanley Marcus*

Here are a couple of examples of innovation that motivated us to switch our buying patterns. One of the great innovations we like is . . .

Bubblegum-Flavored Toothpaste

Bubblegum toothpaste, what a great idea! As parents and grandparents, that's all we buy. Our kids hate the taste of "adult" toothpaste. We also buy them electric toothbrushes in the form of "Spiderman" and other super heroes so they have fun brushing their teeth. It works!

Be careful not to innovate just to look or be different. Innovations must be meaningful to the market with which you are correlated. And also . . .

Beware of the Fickle Factor

I know somebody who doesn't like Wendy's square hamburger patty. The first thing she does is tear off the four points hanging over the edge of the bun. It bugs her! To her, putting a square patty on a round bun is like trying to put a square peg in a round hole. She will shop at Wendy's but those square burgers are not her first choice for that simple reason. Yes, customers are fickle.

Protect yourself against the "fickle factor." Even though your service process is extraordinary and your customers love you, they can be very fickle when somebody comes along with a better idea or a better service concept. Look what happens to established merchants in a community when a Wal-Mart comes to town. And one just did open in our town. Patrons loyal to other stores are now going to Wal-Mart.

Innovation creates new loyalties. I'm even . . .

Fickle About My Pickle

I personally switched pickle brands when Vlasic first started slicing their pickles the long way so they stack better on sandwiches. It was only a little innovation, but it changed my brand loyalty. What one can learn from all this is, when it comes to customer service, little things can mean a lot.

Businesses are living organizations. Like all living things they must adapt to an ever changing environment or die. And, the way businesses adapt is through constant innovation.

Cell phone technology is an example of a field where there is constant innovation. Each company is always trying to out-do the other with innovation. The big innovations were speakerphones, then text messaging capabilities.

Then came the camera phones, then video phones, then phones with "ipod" technology, allowing songs to be downloaded right onto the cell phone. It just keeps going on and on.

So, what about you? I'll bet you can! I'll bet you can think of a number of innovations that persuaded you to change buying patterns. But what have you done in your own company recently that is innovative? List three to six of those innovations below.

Recent innovations in my own organization are:

_____

_____

_____

_____

_____

_____

_____

_____

_____

_____

_____

Business Diagnostics

I have a friend who is a Ph.D. in accounting and years ago he started a company called Business Diagnostics. I was impressed with his approach in helping business owners determine why their company was anemic and sick.

If your business is not doing well, a good place to start is with service diagnostics. Perhaps you'll find it can become vibrant and healthy through the awareness and application of the principles discussed in this book. I certainly hope so.

Let's all join together to help save the world from shoddy customer service. It could make life a little more pleasant. Don't you agree?

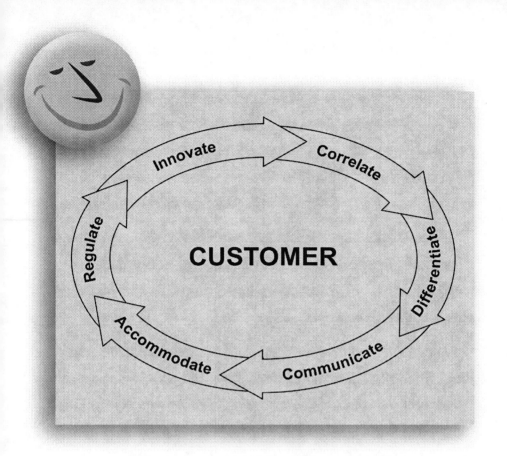

What Gets Focused Upon
Gets Done!

So now what? You have two choices! You can be like the average person that goes through books or workshops and gets excited temporarily, or you can make a resolve to continue to review, practice, and improve your customer service.

Perhaps you can relate to the following learning chart. We submit that when something gets focused upon, it gets attention and can, in many cases, actually improve. For example, when you go through a training course, your performance in that area increases. (See chart.) However, several weeks after the training, be it class, lecture, or book, life continues to throw curve balls your way and your focus on that one thing decreases a little at a time. The result is that your performance declines.

If you focus again on that same topic either through attending another lecture or reviewing the material you studied previously, you are again giving attention to that topic and your performance improves in that area.

Notice that, while there is a decline, refocusing ultimately leads to higher performance each time you re-visit that topic. This is very important to understand. As employers, we need to train our people *regularly* on customer service. As employees, we need to learn and improve continually. The end result is that each individual gets better and better, as does the organization.

Some companies hold training meetings weekly. Others hold training sessions monthly. In deciding what works best for your company, remember the principle conveyed in the title of

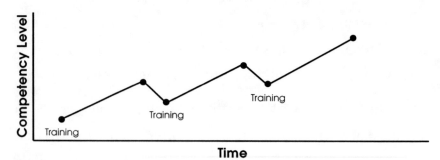

this final chapter: What Gets Focused Upon, Gets Done! This means the more you focus on customer service and make it a priority every day in your business, the greater improvements you will experience.

A word of caution! If you are an employer you may think like the average employer and focus on the labor expense of getting everyone together on a weekly or a monthly basis. That's normal, but very dangerous because it is an inaccurate and short-sighted perception of training. Do not let yourself fall into this trap.

You must think of training as an investment in your employees and ultimately in your company. Spending a little money now on training which increases hourly payroll, yields greater results down the road.

Let me give you another example from our Jamba Juice experience. A few years ago we conducted an experiment on this subject of investing a little extra now for training in hopes of greater rewards in the future.

We began holding regular training classes which were mandatory for all employees. We, of course, paid them for their time which was initially the hardest part to reconcile. After just one meeting we took our customer service scores from 78% to 92% the very next week.

More impressive than a 12% gain in one week's time was that the service and the scores stayed at the higher level over the long term. But there's more . . .

A True Confession

We became complacent and thought we had it all together. We thought we could slow down a bit so we cut training to half the original amount. And guess what happened! That's right! Our customer service scores dropped with the drop in classes.

Because of the nature of the customer service business it is easy to feel overwhelmed by the sheer numbers of transactions entered into each day. We can grow tired of answering the same questions for the hundreds or even thousands of customers we may serve.

To be sure, employees on the front lines day in and day out can tire easily. Keeping them energized with regular training is fundamental to your organization. Commit now to a regular schedule and stick with it.

One more important thing to remember about regular customer service training meetings is this: plan and prepare. If the meetings aren't informative, interactive, upbeat, and different from session to session, your employees will get bored and the training will cease to work for you.

In Conclusion
(or should I say . . . Let's Get Started!?!)

Earlier, in a previous chapter, I discussed the importance of designing your service process. To get you started with a few ideas of what may need to be considered I've decided to include the service outlines for Wm. B. Woods, the upscale women's shoes stores created by my first magnetic customer service tutor, my father – Bill Woods; and for Jamba Juice, the stores successfully owned and operated in the Phoenix area by my son and co-author of this book… the next generation.

Wishing you all the success your customer service people can handle!

Company: Wm. B. Woods
"10 Steps to Sales and Service"

1. Greet and seat the customer

2. Remove the customer's shoes

3. Decide what to show the customer

4. Show the customer the shoes

5. Tell the customer about the shoes

6. Narrow the selection

7. Resolve objections

8. Close the sale

9. Show and sell additional pairs of shoes

10. Establish after-sales rapport

Company: Jamba Juice
"The 6 Customer Service Building Blocks"

1. Greet and engage with each customer within 5 seconds

2. Make great, consistent, healthy products

3. Work together as a team

4. Keep a really clean store

5. Say "Thank you" to each customer

6. Give it a boost – Go the extra mile

Now it is time for you to design your service process. You may have ten steps, six steps, or something in-between. It doesn't matter. Just use the following guidelines and you'll have a plan that is just right for your organization.

- Keep it simple and clear.

- Make sure it is "doable."

    Can this be done with each customer?

    Is it realistic?

- Design it from the customers' perspective.

    What is important to THEM?

- Use an acronym, if possible, to help people remember the steps.

Build upon the concepts outlined in the Circle of Service as they apply uniquely to your business.

The system works!

And—it is the shortest distance to higher sales and higher profits!

Printed in the United States
91039LV00005B/87/A

9 781600 370267